PALINDROME

Grateful Reflections
from the
Home Ground

Tom A. Titus

Coastal
Giant  Press

Cover design by Ana Grigoriu-Voicu at
Books-Design.com

Cover photograph: Mt. Hood from Mirror Lake, Oregon, by Oregon's Mt. Hood Territory
http://www.fhwa.dot.gov/byways/photos/62736

ISBN: 978-1-7333631-1-2

For my father Tom N. Titus,
whose story lives on.

CONTENTS

THANK YOU!

To Kimberlee Wollter, editor, designer, soul mate, and confidant with long-suffering ears for writerly musings and misgivings, you have expanded the possibilities of my world. A sweeping bow goes to my literary cheerleaders in the Red Moons: Grace Elting Castle, Charleynne Gates, Evelyn Hess, Cynthia Pappas, Kay Porter, and Kirsten Steen. Encouragement, ideas, and editorial thoughts came also from Eric Alan, Valerie J. Brooks, John Carter, Martha Gatchell, Melissa Hart, Tracy Miller, Sean Sharp, and Cathy Ward. The poems *Ode to Eight Desert Sunrises* and *Sharpie* were born during a creative arts residency at PLAYA, with special thanks to fellow residents Jennifer Boyden, Rebe Huntman, Olivia Lombardi, and Barbara Rockman, who could see a larger me than fit on my own screen. The poem *Brown* took form on a Working and Writing the Woods workshop sponsored by the Spring Creek Project for Ideas, Nature, and the Written Word. Krystal Abrams cheerfully assisted in developing the icon for Coastal Giant Press.

READ THIS FIRST

Palindromes captivate me. In the strictest sense, a palindrome doesn't inspire awe. It is merely a group of words or letters or numbers that read the same from *start to finish to start*. But artists rarely work within the strictest sense of things. We are more likely to travel to the edges, those fuzzy places that defy sharp definitions, and stare over the brink. When my father left the living world, I allowed myself to become fascinated by the number of palindromes that accompanied his passing. Was I missing something in these idiosyncratic words with *front to back to front* identity? Perhaps. Stare hard at a palindrome, let the words flow *forward then backward then forward* for long enough, and the phrase becomes alive. As with all living things, the edges blur. A palindrome becomes two stink bugs having sex, joined *bug to end to end to bug* for hours in a coupled repetition with no higher aim than making more stink bugs. Yet their coupling is intergenerational and evolutionary; it begins to assume the character of timelessness. Perhaps my father's palindromes only challenged me to notice and reflect on them, to reflect on his life,

1

then begin *that reflection on reflection that* might be the beginning of the infinite.

Human life has an irreversible arrow of time and therefore is not a palindrome. Human lives also become more complex over time. But adding more words or letters or numbers to a palindrome only increases the likelihood that their symmetry will be violated. So palindromes are typically simple. This book *Palindrome* is not a palindrome, nor is it particularly simple. But the individual pieces are short, a collection of interstitial creativity that emerged from within my otherwise frenetic world. They also match my attention span.

On a warm summer day I had a fortuitous encounter with a poet friend that involved a cold beer inside the dim reaches of a pub. The conversation wandered toward William Carlos Williams, the doctor-poet whose name is only one letter shy of being a palindrome. I learned that Williams was a master at using small slices of his day for creative enterprise. Much of the structure of his poetry was defined by fleeting scraps of time when poems could be scribbled between appointments on the back of a prescription pad.

I understand these small snatches of creative work. This is how most of the writings in

Palindrome were born. They are snippets scribbled in my journal at sunrise or words scritched at nightfall on pages becoming dark in the face of an incoming storm. Some were thumb-typed on my phone from night-struck ridges when words struggled for light. Others were penned in tiny script on pieces of folded white paper during noon walks along the Willamette River. And yes, many were typed on a computer at a desk in the way of most modern-day ruminations, often during inky winter mornings before work. In any case, most of these entries originated within small spaces of time.

Each writing embraces a deeply rooted sense of gratitude. This is not a warm and fuzzy version of gratefulness that gushes forth only when all is right. Let's be honest: there is a lot that's wrong in the world. Poet David Whyte refers to gratitude as an *a priori* principle of our existence. What if our gratitude became a bedrock principle of living? This deeper form of gratitude wouldn't be based on what we have, or what has happened around us, or even how we happen to feel in any given moment. It would become a practice, a commitment in our lives. Gratitude would begin to acquire the characteristics of a love relationship.

I love my living relationship with this rainy green crease of the Pacific Northwest. Being alive in this place is a privilege for which I am utterly grateful. I hope that gratitude will seep from these words like clear spring water from an emerald mountain, collecting into a reflective pool within which we might see another world. For your attentive reading, I am also grateful. May Peace find you in any of its multitude of forms.

T.A.T.

LIGHT

~

SHEDDING

I'm rolling south of Saginaw on Interstate 5 on an unusually late start for the Johnny Gunter cabin. An angry sleepless night has left me thin and tired. The weather is changing. A blackberry-tinged sunset sags over the western ridge. Wildfire smoke and incoming clouds churn together. They become the pearlescent interior of an oyster shell arching over toasted rectangles of pasture and ryegrass stretching toward darkening foothills. I say it exhausted. I say it knowing carcinogenic bits of burned tree carbon have infiltrated my eyes and lungs. I say it aloud flying along this flat 65-mile-per-hour car-ridden crayoned line of four-lane asphalt. I say that I am living in the most beautiful place in the world.

Headlights tunnel up the driveway to the cabin, boring into shadows of Douglas-fir and salal. I unlock the old house, take a few things inside, then turn off all the lights. I suppose I should park myself on the porch in lotus position, palms upturned, taking deep meditative breaths. Instead I sit in a cast-off lawn chair, legs stretched outward into blackness. A bourbon bottle balances on a stack of cinder blocks to my right. I take a pull and hope the hot whiskey burn will somehow disinfect my soul. Occasionally this has worked. Darkness presses over my skin, my skin that has become too tight, my skin that is making me itchy and irritable. If only I could shed this thing. I sip and scratch and squirm and sip some more. A cool breeze flows in from the west, rippling over the ridges of my face. The weather is changing.

Morning brings heavy mist. Through the doorway I watch a doe browsing at the edge of the mown meadow, head and legs light and quick. She is the color of desiccated grass, the color of a cougar. She chews a few brown stems of cut knapweed. For no apparent reason she leaps from the ground, jumping quickly to one side, maybe just for the joy of eating wet brown knapweed at the shriveled end of summer. Flat spider webs litter the yard like somber tossed-out plates, every one with a tunnel that disappears into the eternity of a vole hole. Above the old forest, a blue sky crack drifts casually toward the sun. Gray light transforms into silver. Spider plates glisten, each sequined with a thousand tiny droplets of captured mist. The weather has changed. My skin does not itch.

SHOW ME MY WORDS

On winter mornings I awaken early while the sun sleeps in. I feed the cats, light the woodstove, make my coffee. Then I systematically shut off all the lights except a halogen lamp on its long black insect leg that reaches from a mahogany shelf to throw a bright bubble around my overstuffed chair. My backside sinks into the putty-colored cushions, back inside the yolky softness of a hopeful leathery egg buried in sand on a sun-warmed beach. In this upright embryonic state, incubated by the flickering woodstove, a mantra seeps out on a small exhalation of carbon dioxide and unused oxygen, air I no longer need for anything except to float one phrase: show me my words.

I love other people's words: words in song, words in stories, words in poetry, words of human discourse, words about words. But please. Show me *my* words, on this morning, in this small sphere of light cast by a phony sun in the dead of winter, darkness ceding to the watery dimness of another downpour. Show me my words. Because those words are already waiting inside, strung in sentences like genes coiled into chromosomes, ready to be unwound, switched on, expressed as something new in the world, hatched into the wide-eyed morning.

Show me my words while my beautiful white-haired grandson sleeps. He had a tough night. He can say "chromosome." But his utterances are few and lack depth, nuance, and context. His words are disjointed clusters of cells insufficient to describe the full animal of pain that settled into his body at bedtime. For this he had only screams and the spasmodic arch of his two-year-old torso. His adults could only surround him with love, wring their hands, make phone calls, try to decide what next. He decided for them. Some portion of his pain finally wandered into the night, and he fell into an exhausted sleep. Jackets were removed, car keys placed back in the car key bowl. When he awoke an hour later he cried, but his back was not arched. He woke again, but his crying was only fussing. Then we slept.

Show me my words. Because I need to tell you, dearest offspring of my offspring, that most pain is like this. I need to tell you that on those days when the warm egg of your life is pierced by needles of ice, the sun will rise, burn through the clouds, and melt those stabbing crystals. Show me the words to tell you that someday, even in the immediacy of your anguish, you will know the hope of having your pain in the past. Your hope is as real as your life on this outrageous life-infested rock hurtling through the void.

Show me my words. Please.

ODE TO EIGHT DESERT SUNRISES

1
Silver and rose rainbow trout ribbon shimmers across russet hills. Pink flesh sizzles over your orange coals.

2
How *did* you squeeze raspberry jam from that short stack of cloud pancakes? Damn. I've forgotten my fork.

3
Another newborn wonder, pink baby's butt bulge becoming an amber birthstone spilling across blond desert.

4
Dying crescent Moon sits upright in a prickly bed of stars. Her last breath tickles your warm arms. New text from Boston. My wife's mother has died.

5

Gray Fox sky stalks from behind Winter Ridge, rushes out, drapes you in his silver pelt. You become an old soul, impervious to opinion, unwilling to compete.

6

An incoming storm has stirred you into a stunning mess. May I clean your bloody wrists, bandage you in cloud wrack, mop the stains of your beautiful chaos from the low ridge?

7

If I were in you and you in me, then maybe our conjoined light might push this darkening sky, this pummeling wind, out of the valley.

8

Repetition makes your daily miracle less miraculous, each morning a little later, a little farther south. Willows become lonely, fade to sunflower. We are missing you.

TIDE OF DUSK

Dusk drifts like dust onto the mown meadow. The lawn tractor is shut down and loaded into the old white trailer. But stillness is not silence. Raven growls from somewhere up the valley, her motive black and opaque, perhaps announcing the end of a good carcass-filled day. Nighthawk is diving, arresting his hell-bent trajectory with a buzzing *whoosh* that sounds like a shorting electrical wire. All the while Swainson's Thrush throws his burbling song toward the creamy mote of a quarter moon slipping toward the western ridge. The faint olfactory footfall of cut grass rises on a wispy onshore breeze wafting east from the Pacific.

Somewhere in the growing shadows creeps a hint of sorrow: small, furtive, untraceable. It slips like a doe from darkening conifers, nimble across the freshly cut field. I sense this melancholy, but not with eyes or ears or nose. It rises to the surface of my mind like the evening dimple of a feeding trout.

Our society has a strange relationship with sorrow. We treat it like a jacket stain, something to be ignored or removed by any means neces-

14

sary. We subvert it by shopping or subtle substance abuse or any of a plethora of digital distractions. This makes me sad. Because sadness is a recognition that something of value is missing from our lives. Sadness does not preclude contentment or perhaps even happiness. Sorrow is an emotion worthy of our wrapped arms.

I'm staring at that lunar crescent slung in the dusking sky and thinking of my snowy-haired grandson born on a waxing June moon. Even then I knew ours would be a long-distance love affair. I'm wistful because he lives in a faraway place and wasn't here today to pick the first blueberries and eat canned chili for dinner. This is a tiny star of sadness in the vast constellation of sadnesses in the world. Even so, here in the rising darkness, I'm wondering what sort of love would have me happy that he is 3,000 miles away. What beautiful irony. My contentment with ripe blueberries rolling in my fingers and damp newborn air swelling into the growing moon is what sends this small sorrow drifting in on the flowing tide of dusk.

BLACK IN THIRD PERSON

He arrived at the cabin in late afternoon in the season when afternoons flicker and die like tiny winter midges. All that remained of that hottest driest summer were blackened tomato plants sagging in their rusty cages and moldering corn stalks twined with brittle bean vines. Dead plants were stacked across the garden beds in a pyre of decomposition that would nurture new life in the spring.

At dusk the storm slouched just off the coast, a beast with humid breath flooding eastward across darkening canyons and ridges. Stalking rain tasted like the acrid seep of a lead fishing weight squeezed between his teeth. Ragged clouds sailed in the dying light, battleship wraiths strewn across the western sky. Why had they come, these vaporous shadows of war? Were they running from a fight lost long ago? Or were they harbingers of a new war, sailing toward the prospect of new blood? He willed them back toward the steel heave of the Pacific. But the storm was strong, indifferent to his existence.

Darkness engulfed the front porch. There were no streetlights houselights headlights holiday lights. Only a trifling bubble of brightness from his headlamp kept him from drowning in astronomical events utterly beyond his control. Raindrops ticked against the pickup. He wrote in black ink in a black journal in black night stirred by a black breeze sighing through ancient trees on the ridge. He wrote hoping this crushing blackness would squeeze some essence from him that had been diluted by an overly busy autumn.

Finally, he flinched. Wind and darkness and solitude quickly overwhelmed the small glow of the headlamp, overwhelmed the small glow of his spirit. He packed his journal and shards of the broken bulb of his soul. Inside the house, he switched off the headlamp, hung it from a nail, fumbled for the house keys, locked the door by Braille.

Fists of rain pummeled the pickup as he drove up the road to Martha and Jerry's. Their kitchen was happy and warm with dinner. Together they drank wine, listened to the pounding rain. As he left their house, the storm began to gather him in. He looked back. Light from the kitchen window pushed gently against his face. A smile cracked the darkness.

ETCH A SKETCH

Newborn crescent moon arced toward the orange horizon, earliest sunset in this season of early sunsets. By morning, clouds the color and texture of untrowelled concrete were poured between flanking foothills. A charcoal skein of Canada Geese quivered eastward across Etch A Sketch gray. For some goosely reason, they wavered, broke ranks. I understand. Here at the somber end of a year when our spring is drying and trees are dying and democracy seems as shallow as a Russian Facebook feed or a Big Oil lobbyist, here in this season of darkness just before Light returns, my Etch A Sketch knobs are twirling. The geese restored their wandering line. The verdict is out on humanity. I went to work anyway.

BREATH

~

STARSTRUCK

Morning at the cabin began a little rough around the edges. While making my way to the door with a coffee and my journal, I shifted the thermos into my right hand to turn the knob. The lid came off and the coffee ended up on the floor. The floor is old and rough and dry, and it drank half the coffee before I could mop it up. I didn't know a house could be so thirsty.

Out on the front porch, fresh coffee in hand and the meadow glowing like a perfectly toasted marshmallow, I need to tell you about last night's stars. I talked late into the night with a friend, sipped bourbon from an insulated coffee mug, inhaled sorrow, breathed out the best love I knew. On my return to the cabin, the pickup was engulfed by the tree tunnel of the driveway, then spit like a slippery pit into the grassy parking area. I silenced the engine, quieted the noisy shine of headlights. The door creaked into darkness on dusty hinges. I stood and leaned into the cool metal fender, pressed my face upward.

Lights from town kept their distance. Moon was on holiday. The sky was a star-shot ceiling fringed by tattered silhouettes of fir limbs and conifer ridges, as though I was inside the gaping

21

maw of the valley looking outward into space. The Milky Way was a glittering brushstroke smeared across stellar chaos. Above the shadows of old trees on the ridge, I found the North Star, a pushpin anchoring Ursa Minor to the blackboard of space. Small Bear poured the infinite contents of his heart into Ursa Major, the two of them never to be united. The vastness was staggering. Slowly, gently, I shook my head, pulled the starshine air deeply into my lungs.

A long time ago, in a place near the center of the continent, I gazed into a night sky arching deep and wide and unfettered. I stared too long. The rumpled edge of infinity tripped me up. I stumbled, then caught myself just above the boundless maw, my young mind frozen by the stare of absolute nihilism. Sometimes I'm a slow learner. But I can be taught. Never again will I step to the edge of that precipice. Never.

Yes, we are specks in space and time. Yes, we are in all probability alone in this moment. But our tiny loneliness is a reason for being. We are the voice of consciousness in the universe. The unending stars tell us our time to sing is short. Our time was short from the beginning.

RIPENING SKY

Finally, another evening on the porch. The berries are picked. Barn Swallows cut arcs around the sickle moon, slicing pieces from a blueberry pie sky. My chest rises and drops, a deep slow exhalation, the first one in weeks, a breath that holds nothing back, empties my lungs with complete faith that my diaphragm will contract downward and inhale the sunset. The old forest exhales, too. A wave of cool air pushes across the meadow and laps against the right side of my face.

Again I breathe. Reclusive thoughts emerge that have hidden in old green canyons incised in my mind by the relentless water of living. In my marathon of busy-ness, this spring I finally hit the wall. I have been damned, and not by the gods or uncontrollable circumstances, although these may have played their part. Mostly I am cursed by choice, by my own pressing need to do stuff. A lot of stuff. All of the time.

Another deep breath. Probably I could foist some responsibility onto genetics, an inherited brain chemistry that requires constant stimulation, a skinny loping coyote mentality, pressed onward by a barely coherent feeling that it's harder to hit a moving target.

I have enough gray matter remaining to make other choices. I own my busy-ness. And now I will own this stillness, this next breath of quiet cooling air, this darkness climbing onto big fir trees on the ridge, this brightening Moon sliding toward the western edge of my world, hanging in the ripening sky.

QUIET

The gentling sounds of New Year's Eve morning swirl inside the cabin. Woodstove whispers and creaks. Fly snaps out of torpor, buzzes in rare winter warmth. Beyond thin windows, Steller's Jay squawks from conifers straining upward through the foggy mystery of morning.

In our manufactured world, quiet is rare in any form. Holiday noise is especially incessant: cars, trains, planes, phones, people talking yelling singing snoring, parties, shopping, resolutions, televisions blooming with Rose Bowl, Orange Bowl, Participation Ribbon Bowl.

Wise Teachers have for ages told us that quiet is an internal state, portable into all external circumstances. I'm not that highly evolved. Noise is an addiction that stretches the skin of my soul to the point that I am in danger of disappearing with a *BANG* or a slow withering leak. From somewhere beyond conscious recognition I find myself thirsty for a long cool drink of quiet. Occasionally an intervention becomes necessary. I send myself to the hills.

In this place, quiet is more than silence, more than not-sound. Quiet is a liquid. I can

25

drink it, bathe in it. Quiet is a gas I draw into the wet recesses of my lungs. Quiet is stillness, an absence of busy-ness, space between noise, pause between heartbeats, blackness between stars, the exuberant rotting of winter leaves. If I were a torrent salamander with skin and gills constantly bathed and breathing in a cool pool of quiet, would quiet even have a name?

Here I can stretch my arms, gather in the quiet. I'm grateful for fly buzz and jay squawk, the pause before another life-giving inhalation.

RUMPLE OF DARKNESS

Somewhere in the dark space between my diaphragm and liver lives a wild thing. He loves to run. He's getting a little old and thin around the edges, but sometimes he still loves to run hard. So on Tuesdays I open the gate and turn him loose. He and I run free and headlong for no reason other than the sheer animal joy of unfettered movement and open pores and long muscles relaxed by exhaustion. We plod back to the gym on a well-used path that wriggles in right angle turns through a shady cemetery, a trail respectful of graves and those who no longer run. We juxtapose our loping body above the dead. We feel very alive.

My Tuesday trips through this graveyard are brief and superficial, at least for the time being. Here on the daylight side of the dirt, I'm unaccustomed to visits by the dead. I'm especially unaccustomed to seeing these particular dead. They are too damned smart to die by the usual means—cars, cats, windows, power lines, and bird-snatching hawks. But here he was—a sprawl of wet black feathers, still shiny even in subdued light beneath big Douglas-firs. A crow, dead as a dark stone.

I want to believe this crow didn't die alone. I like the idea that his buddies were with him high in the fir limbs, all of them hunched against a January storm. When the wet wind became too much, his nictitating membranes slid like gray shades over each bronze eye. Blackness enveloped blackness. Ebony feet relaxed and relinquished the branch to winter. His lifeless body landed with a muffled *plop* in needle duff, right wing outstretched, head cocked, left side dirt down, dark beak closed forever.

When I was young I stalked a flock of crows from cottonwoods along the river bottom, dark birds scattered like basalt cobbles across corn stubble. I remember a feral surge of joy from the airborne crumple of dusky feathers meeting birdshot. There must be a hundred reasons to hate these big-brained wise-ass eaters of songbird nestlings and basking garter snakes, raucous hawk mobbers, stealers of unguarded submarine sandwiches. But I'm done with all that. My self-righteous bloodlust has evaporated, partly with age, partly with bookish knowledge. Crows are just too damned smart. Do you know what I mean?

Now I'm a funny old guy with skin wide open and oozing sweat, visiting the dead in mid-day dusk. I stand with reaching hand cupped downward over this damp rumple of darkness, maybe in a blessing, maybe catching a last wisp of life or the cool breath of hollow-boned death rising into conifers.

My tired animal and I jog on, grateful to be dodging headstones.

OPEN YOUR SKIN

Coastal mountains stretch along the western edge of North America like an undulating salamander, green and moist and cool. Perch somewhere along her spine. Make yourself small and unnoticeable. Become dark and still on a winter evening when night seeps in like cold spring water. You feel the rise and fall of her breathing, slow and intermittent, barely perceptible, as though breathing were optional, and she could inhale the universe through conifer skin covering the ridges of her ribs and vertebrae.

After you become tiny and alone, let your eyes close in the easy darkness. Notice that each subtle breath of these mountains is really a summation of many small breaths: inhalations of moss, sword fern, salal; becoming larger: vine maple, yew, cascara; becoming still larger: western hemlock, Douglas-fir, red cedar. There are exhalations of elk, bear, deer; becoming smaller: mountain beaver, rough-skinned newt, Pacific Wren; becoming still smaller: centipede, millipede, longhorn beetle; becoming microscopic: protozoa and bacteria more numerous than stars in the universe stretching infinitely away above black ridges.

30

You are very small. Perhaps you are discomfited by your inconsequential existence. You might pretend to be large. This is of no real help. The vastness of these heaving mountains, the sheer weight of their being and all the beings that reside within them is overwhelming. You might try to disappear. This is of no help either. Cold air on your cheeks, the smell of winter leaf rot, twitter of a Screech Owl from the valley bottom, or maybe the cold seep of pain from an arthritic joint are reminders of your one-and-only existence.

Recognize that you squirm for a reason. It is the illusion of your separate life. There is only one remedy for your insignificance. Take a breath. Inhale the swirl of oxygen gifted by slowly breathing conifers. Feel each molecule cling to the iron redness of your blood. Let your steamy exhalation join the vapor emanating from wet nostrils of the pregnant doe bedded at the base of a rotting stump. This collective outward rush forms a vast pool of carbon dioxide, a reciprocal offering to the trees.

Then do one more thing. Open your skin to the universe. You will expand to the measure of your awareness.

WATER

~

BEAVER POOL

The olallieberries were picked by the time the round blue thermometer on the front porch headed northward of 90 degrees. Respite lay in a quiet pool in the creek, a place a few miles downstream where last year the beaver built a dam that backed the water into a respectable swimming hole. In this far upstream world, 4 feet deep qualifies as respectable. For various reasons, beaver don't last long around here, so I had no expectation that the dam remained.

The pickup found its ever hopeful way from the shadowed foot of the driveway down the road to the gravel pullout. A well-worn path knew the route to the stream. Indolent air was goaded by an acrid flush of nettle and salmonberry. Standing on the bank, I stared into tannin water. From the creek bottom black eyes of basalt cobble stared back. Peeled sticks spread like a pale hand along the dark belly of the stream. The beaver were still there. Half a dozen finger-size trout fanned their fins in languid water. Every so often a fish dimpled the surface, slurped a floating insect, darted downward, disappeared into alder shadow.

I slid out of shoes, shorts, and shirt. My feet picked their way down the prickly bank. Cool creek skin slid around me. I gasped, caught my breath, stroked upstream, turned to float on my back. Salmonberries and slow water licked at my nakedness. Salty summer drifted silently downstream.

SPAWNED OUT

The afternoon sky has grown weary of raining. A steely sea of overcast ruptures into vaporous breakers crashing silently against steep ridges. Insipid sunlight occasionally peeks through, but Sun seems tired as well. Hermit Thrush twitches his russet tail from a bare hazel branch. Normally I visit this place in February. But spawning Coho have been calling to me, and I am compelled to come in December.

Coho are the iconic salmon of the Oregon Coast Range. Their cousins the Chinook are larger, more powerful, perhaps more charismatic. But Chinook lack the staying power of Coho, who are uniquely adapted to spawning in filamentous tributaries deep in the coastal mountains. Coho are smaller and arrive later in the fall when lower order streams are made accessible by the swelling rains. Ample winter flows keep spawning gravels submerged until the eggs hatch and their captive embryos are freed to negotiate the vicissitudes of rising and falling water. This fluctuating upstream world is better suited to nimble endurance than to raw power.

I grab an orange-handled machete from behind the seat of the pickup. Surely by now the old roadbed in the bottom of the canyon has been swallowed by Armenian blackberry brambles. But more years have passed than I realize, and the trail is mostly clear. Douglas-fir in the clearcut have grown tall enough to block the sunlight, and the blackberries are being killed by shade. So goes the ruthless and relentless succession of plant communities. Even invasive blackberries can be strangled.

At the end of the road, the Douglas-fir canopy is completely closed. Dark duff covers the forest floor, interrupted only by a host of slouching mushrooms rotting back into the nutrient cycle. From here, I follow a game trail across the lower end of a newer clearcut. The fir have doubled in height since my last trip. These trees were planted to cover the cost of logging. I'm sure the land would be better left to its own processes, but I'm unsure of where I would get lumber.

Beyond this clearcut lies a native forest two centuries old. Some Douglas-fir trunks are 4 feet in diameter, their bark furrowed by dark canyons 6 inches deep. Pileated Woodpecker has excavated a fresh 4-inch oblong hole at the base of one trunk. Inside the grove, the meager light dims. Soft creek music rises from my left. I descend to the bank and stand above a clearing stream coursing along a shallow rill of blond sandstone cobbles. Very recently the flow was much higher. A small sandbar is scrubbed clean and devoid of tracks. I step into the flow with impunity, thankful for knee-high rubber boots, and immediately begin looking for evidence of spawning Coho. A light-colored scrap undulates in a milky blue pool just upstream of my ford. Focusing hard, I finally discern a piece of old man's beard lichen attached to a submerged fir limb, waving in the current like the scarred tail of a ravaged salmon.

Climbing from the stream bed, I negotiate the thick understory. This forest is perennially wet, lush with salal, sword fern, and old-growth vine maple. Large conifers lie haphazardly in various stages of decay. My body reminds me of the flow of time—ducking under vine maple and crawling over down logs is more of a chore than I remember. Yet persistence seems a worthy endeavor. I choose a route for keeping the stream in view. The narrow creek is clearing from the recent rain, so fish or freshly churned gravel in the spawning redds should be easy to spot. The stream meanders along the flat canyon floor, forming quiet pools in crooked elbows, potential resting places for spent salmon. But this after-noon there is only the liquid rattle of moving wa-ter, the swish of wet brush against rain pants.

People have been here before me. Pieces of pink flagging along the creek mark summer snorkel surveys for smolts. An ugly orange sign with curling edges is tacked to a large hemlock. In black letters it proclaims SALMON SPAWN-ING SURVEY, as though this matters to any-one or anything but me or the spawning survey-ors. Still, I appreciate that someone cares, even if their trail is marked in dayglow pink.

I continue upstream. My need to visit these salmon is a strange compulsion that is difficult to articulate. I can say only that these trips seem to meet a need to become a part of the world that still makes sense. Clouds relent. Sun breaks briefly through. The rare December sunset lies far to the south, so Sun shines into the south-facing canyon mouth. Soon the diminishing light presses in. A warm cabin is waiting back up the road. I should turn back. But I can't.

Finally, the canyon relinquishes. On a freshly scrubbed sandbar perhaps 6 feet long rests a small litter of bones. Toothy lower jaws and bony gill plates are scattered around the core of a skull. The skull is attached to vertebrae that remain strung together by bleached-out sinew and muscle fibers. A curve of needle-like ribs sweeps downward from the vertebrae into the sand. The entire array of bones is bent into a shallow, upwardly bending arc. High rainfall earlier in the fall has already provided the necessary water for spawning. Long before my arrival this afternoon, the Coho had taken care of their reproductive business, the business prescribed by evolution.

On the surface, all that remains are remains. No one can know whether this salmon found a mate and successfully spawned. The only certainty is that orange flesh has melted into the creek or been scavenged by raccoons. This fish has become part of a larger cycle in which ocean nutrients are tethered to the reproductive will of the Coho and transported far upstream into forest ecosystems. The continuation of this story, the one now ending at dusk in a scatter of cloudy bones, becomes an article of faith. I choose to believe this salmon parented a clutch of fertile eggs nestled somewhere in the sandstone gravel. Inside each translucent capsule, a twitching embryo awaits its time to hatch and renew the cycle of growing smolts descending Smith River to become new nickel silver flashing through schools of Pacific baitfish. I imagine my own aging body 4 years from now, struggling through

41

wet fall underbrush, trying to intercept the on-going circles of ocean, rain, creek, and Coho. This is my version of hope.

ATMOSPHERIC RIVER

Bedroom window cracked open to
atmospheric river, ocean river,
sky river, cloud river streaming.

So many ways to hear …
every drop a click of rain
music back of mouth of tongue of ears.

Marine air, damp pheromone of leaf
rot, muddy horse prints, ditches
brimful with breeding chorus frogs.

Nostrils hit flood stage, olfactory neurons
fire, flush neurotransmitters
into neuronal spaces.

Hiss of rain serpent slithering east,
gravity-borne water sluicing across
leaves shingles streets, becoming
small waterfalls breaking over
precipice of sleep.

So many ways to drown.

OPEN TRAIL

TRAIL CLOSED. Red capital letters shout from the edge of the quieting forest. Some say I'm deep, some say I'm troubled, and a few say I'm deeply troubled. I just say yes and walk past the sign.

A thin path threads a carpet of sword fern and bunchberry spread under cool morning shadows of old Douglas-fir. I turn toward the creek and settle my butt on a cushion of dry moss. Thimbleberry canes rise from this softness, leaves like splayed palms, some holding wide-eyed five-petaled stars, others with green thumbnail berries anticipating the ripening summer. A dwarf Oregon grape leaf prickles my right leg.

Breathe. Open. Above the hurrying stream, a yellow salamander of sunlight slips through, becomes a squirming green scatter amid alder leaves. Dappled water dashes over ochre stones, scatter of cold volcano bones. Jumbled creek music surges above tumbling water. Higher frequencies rise to the top, float somewhere above bumblebee buzz but beneath the highest note of Swainson's Thrush, whose liquid call lifts toward the ridge. Water bulges and breaks over a large stone, becoming a soothing midrange burble before running headlong into a fallen fir.

In the lower register lies an intermittent gurgle, as though the stream is clearing her throat. The rumble settles in my chest. It is the subtle admonishment of an elder asking that I open myself to spacious uncluttered voice. Uncluttered but not uncomplicated. I'm breathing in this place as an unlikely outcome of three generations of "wood product" livelihoods that cling to me like that moss cap on the decaying stump across the creek, its rotten brick-red face staring. Spires of old Douglas-fir, limbless for 100 feet, pierce the blue band of sky. I see those trees lying in state, bound to log trucks headed for a mill far from this canyon, ready for precision transformation by laser driven saws into high-grade yellow lumber smelling of sweet turpentine. I can never be unlogged.

Again the creek clears her throat. Yes, I am of logging. But my days have become a healing clearcut, new trees with roots pushing down, canopy casting upward and outward, growing into stability and shade, becoming a mixed forest, complex in space and time. I am the deepening wild, woven needles and dank dead wood and aching water bathing gills of Coastal Giant

45

Salamanders and sucker-mouthed tadpoles of Tailed Frogs. I am fingers stiffening with age and morning cold. I am an open trail.

RISE AND FALL

Five a.m. and I am thirsty for the music of rain. My house is tight, with a heavily insulated ceiling and high-R windows. But I barely hear the rain. I pull on a puffy jacket and warm hat, slip out the back door into damp darkness, and settle into a cold metal lawn chair under the awning.

The rain is steadying but not steady. Beneath the driving downpour lives a subtle undercurrent, a gentle undulation that feels like my wet breathing, inhalation less intense, exhalation slightly more forceful. Unimpeded drips form a round rattle on the polycarbonate roof, interspersed with deeper more resonant drops that fall from bare branches of the cherry tree reaching into the darkness, stretching toward spring.

I miss the ticks and plops of forest rain. But this morning I'm grateful to be dry, relieved that eventually I can rise from this metallic chill seeping into my backside, slide back inside the warm womb of my house, the soft nest of my easy chair by the woodstove.

The physicality of falling rain seems a little miraculous. Individual water molecules are slightly unbalanced by shared quantum forces of the two hydrogen atoms and an oxygen atom. Each hydrogen is a little positive, the oxygen a little negative. Opposites attract. Molecules become gregarious because hydrogens of one molecule are drawn to the oxygen of another. But heat makes them brave and they separate, rising like tiny angels into the atmosphere.

Eventually cooler air causes them to huddle in droplets too large to remain airborne. They become fallen angels that sing to me from my patio roof. These once-heavenly hosts stream together into drainpipes into gutters into Amazon Creek into Willamette and Columbia Rivers into Pacific Ocean.

Rise and fall of tides. Rise of vapor and fall of drumming rain. Rise and fall of my chest, of words on a dark morning.

ON LOOKOUT CREEK

My tent was taut above the urgent stream. The nearest neighbors were an ancient yew and Douglas-fir, nearly touching one another, certainly intertwined and sharing from their roots. Yew was likely the same age as Fir but a fraction of his size. While Fir soared toward the sun, Yew was content to make do with a gnarled and shadowed existence. Yet Yew had the ironwood heart: springy, resilient, stuff of native bows, feller of elk and deer.

Three weeks after knee surgery, I had overdone it. Sleep was fitful, painful at times. I ignored that analgesic rush of water, white noise expanding into blackness, didn't think to let the soothing music of the stream flow through my swollen knee and carry away my mental embrace of pain. Instead, I became my pain, waking with every change of position, finally not waking because there was no sleep.

Daylight seeped in. My aching leg picked its way down the rocky creek bank. Sitting on a boulder, I dangled my throbbing knee over the smooth bulge of cool basalt. I did not feel my age. I felt older. Older than weathered river stones but not nearly so smooth, older than last night's stars but not nearly as bright. A cup of warmed-over coffee thick enough to spread on toast leaned against the rock. I sipped gratefully. This helped.

Morning sun drifted over the eastern ridge, sifting onto green-needled tops of Old Ones towering above the stream. For a moment there was only a single sound, a deep gurgle and flush from the broken silver-gray ribbon of water. Alder trunks were silver-gray also, vertical representations of the rock-strewn creek. A huge Douglas-fir log lay just downstream, cracked open from its fall across the creek, heart rotten and red and bared to the eyes of the living, to the rush and reach of water and alder.

Water Ouzel bobbed on a midstream boulder, gray bird on gray rock. The short needle of its beak probed the glistening stone for food that was invisible to me. Earlier it had fluttered downstream with its mate. Perhaps this was he, and she was tucked with nestlings in a cozy cavity in the bank, warming them while he hunted and gathered, picked and pecked for wet bug bits to regurgitate for nearly fledged young. Or maybe I'm inventing too honorable a story for him. Maybe this was she, investing her all into those babies while he grabbed an indolent nap on a downstream rock. I hoped the coffee would make me more charitable.

Sun rose steadily, pushing his yellow light downward over dinosaurian trunks. My coffee grew cold. I rose. Unsteadily. My aged knee had gifted me with newborn empathy. This morning my heart was with the gnarled yew, the cracked and rotten log. I struggled up the bank, back to my tent, my cereal. My ibuprofen.

BEINGS

~

PRELUDE TO HEAT

A bird-sung morning cracked open and spread, yellow and cool, across the meadow. Birds sing when it's cool because singing is hard work. They know that an avalanche of heat is rumbling toward us off a high-pressure ridge in the north. Spotted Towhee lacerates the air with a wheezy buzz from the healing clearcut next door. Band-tailed Pigeon casts down a low *whoo-hoooo* from high on the western ridge. Our Barn Swallow family leaps from the power line to chitter and slice to their mud nest in the garage. Raven utters a series of rapid croaks. Raven repeats.

Faint mist lifts from the valley floor toward the house, spirit of the dying night. Dove-gray vapor carries the damp *coo* of ozone into my nose, a wet granularity that reminds me of dust. Sunlight breaks over eastern hills, imposes its orange sheen onto ridges prickled with dark conifers.

I listen into my chest. Inside, there is nothing as interesting as this unfolding day. Only inconsequential musings of meadow now browning, picking berries ahead of the heat, tomorrow's class that I could teach in my sleep. No cumulus of easily characterized emotion puffs into this introspective gaze. I am only shifting mist, mown grass drying in a warming breeze, softly settling.

Maybe this low buzz of emotion is the sound of Peace. When whatever-I-would-have-done-or-will-do-or-might-be-doing drifts away, becomes formless mist floating up from the creek. When inside becomes outside. When my song is no longer mine.

SHARPIE

Sharp-shinned Hawk
is hawking fall warblers from
willows fading yellow above
the iron pond. On my
porch railing he stands with
steely back and rusty breast
ruffling in an icy breeze.
Willow-lance talons clench a
wad of ashen feathers. His
bloodshot stare is clear.
He doesn't give a shit about
my opinion on matters of
life or death, particularly in
October. I stare back, tell him
I don't give a shit about his.
I'm not bitter. He's just
making wages. When I
glance away he melts,
leaving in that
death-struck space three
gray-sky tufts of warbler
down drifting north.

RESTLESS

If T.S. Eliot was right and April really is the cruelest month, then surely September qualifies as the most restless.

On a Sunday afternoon trip to the Johnny Gunter cabin, I rounded a bend on Upper Smith River Road. Ahead was a large lump of coal-colored feathers stretched prone near the centerline. "Large dark bird" was all my mind could register, so I hung a U-turn to investigate. It was a Turkey Vulture. They make a decent living foraging roadkill of various sorts, but I've never seen one who had died in the process. I couldn't leave its elegant naked-headed body to be mutilated beneath the tires of Monday morning log trucks. Yet a full burial seemed inappropriate given Turkey Vulture culture and evolution. I dragged its stiffening corpse off the road and down the bank a bit, where it could become a strand in the local food web—perhaps dinner for a scavenging skunk or raccoon or bear.

At the cabin, the sunburned meadow stretched like a tawny cat beneath a robin's egg sky. But the robin's nest was empty. Barn Swallows no longer swooped and chittered into their mud cups clinging to the rafters of the garage.

Last weekend I knew they were gone because the sky was carved by arcing Violet-Green Swallows. Had the Barn Swallows been there, they would have muscled the Violet-Greens out of their airspace. From the dirt floor of the garage, I gathered piles of swallow poop into a bucket. These processed remains of a zillion mosquitos would fertilize the garlic bed later this fall.

Also gone were the musical thermals of Swainson's Thrushes, as though the air had become too dry and warm to carry them. Instead, an arid cloud of cricket music buzzed above the seed heads of meadow knapweed next door. I keep the knapweed mowed on our side of the meadow, but clearly the crickets prefer those tall unkempt weeds on the neighbor's place. Crickets don't give a flip if knapweed is introduced and invasive. They've made their peace with this hybrid landscape.

Desiccation has its place, even in the garden. Bean plants were becoming jaundiced. I removed their lifeline of spring water to allow the pods to ripen and cure. Painted Mountain corn was ready to shuck and leave to dry on the stalks. The ripping sound of violated ears broke the breeze that broomed the conifer boughs.

Twilight. Wind faltered, whisked away to some distant place. Stars blinked open, uninhibited in the black new moon sky. Even Moon needs to rest occasionally.

I've always become unspeakably restive in this indecisive space between summer and autumn. A long time ago September gave me butterflies. Not this evening. My bones are hollowing in the dying light, but I've become too old to fly, too rooted. Peace must find me here on the ground, inhaling cricket song.

FEATHER

Red-tailed Hawk left a tail feather for me at the spring, disembodied, more delicate even than moss and trickling water. On the quill was a snowy puff of down, becoming straight-edged and russet, laddered with dark bands, each a wavering silhouette of wings on wind, soaring toward a white tip. On a morning with a rocky start, the feather was a gift of softness given by Hawk as a token of freedom from the gravity of circumstances. But it was not mine. Carrying it away would have been wrong in the strictly legal sense. But higher laws were in play. The feather belonged in this earthbound place, meant for me only as witness to its placement on moss encircling clear water, meant for me to breathe a moment of silky beauty into a hard-edged morning, meant for me in the truest sense of ownership— to be shared with Deer Mouse, Black Bear, Calypso Orchid, Old Fir, and every other being inhabiting this shadowed forest.

MY FRIEND ASKED

how I could possibly love October. I suppose
because it is:

a coastal valley inundated by a tsunami of even-
ing light, heartbreakingly yellow except that your
heart was broken three times earlier that day by
75 blue-eyed degrees, a carefree sea lion surfing
dreadlock curls, a chipmunk skull she slipped
into your empty mushroom basket,

red clown tears of vine maple who know they
will soon become November gnomes, naked
and twisted beneath overlords of fir and hem-
lock,

that first gentle please-bring-more rain to mois-
ten drought-stricken duff, tender not-really-
enough rain for salmon to run for sex to die, or
swell the shriveled chanterelles and papery moss
hiding a chalky elk bone,

a torrent of apples rumbling from wheelbarrow
to homemade wooden boxes,

a reckless lover you should have left long ago but need their energy even though they always dump you heartbroken in a November downpour,

an anxiety dream that leaves you beached and salty and sad and glad it's over but wondering why it came,

shrinking days and stretching darkness that tinker with your brain chemistry and make you hope to live then someday die under October sun orange through closed lids.

BROWN

Brown is a color never written. Brown is thesaurus bait: auburn, brunette, bronze, coffee, russet; a Wikipedia entry: beaver, beige, buff, chestnut, chocolate, cocoa, khaki, tan, taupe, walnut.

Brown is cutting new trail along Shotpouch Creek, buried beneath a mountain of uncaring greens who don't give a woodrat's ass about Wikipedia, cradled in a canyon of Calypso Orchid, Bleeding Heart, and graves of children with no more choices.

Brown is rain-swollen water polishing sandstone cobbles, rollicking hard against the newly fallen alder soon to feel the scratch of a hummocking mink, drawn for peculiar lithe reasons to the opposite bank.

Brown is the ferocious chatter of Pacific Wren asserting his walnut-size presence inside unforged blades of sword fern, clasp of newts nestled in drippy ponds, sideband snail backpacking a spiral galaxy.

Brown is blackberry root in churned soil, waiting on fading footfall, poised to engulf this human trace in a tsunami of thorny futility.

Brown is my grandson's eyes, obsidian pupils, black holes capturing light within his year-old countenance, too dark for a white man's world.

Brown is the color his brother cannot be, broken pigment gene gifting blizzard hair blowing over eyes of aged glacier ice, incandescent smile warming a face too white for a white man's world.

Brown is an arthritic shoulder, fulcrum for this heavy hoe, swing, drop, and chop signaling limitless days now limited, return to the churn of granular earth, riot of rot, rain to dimple other faces, creek song for other ears, end of this white man's world.

WILD THING

I don't have time for this sentimentality. The pruning isn't finished, and early spring buds on the real apple trees verge on bursting.

But here you are, growing on the wild side of the orchard fence, feral adolescent with no decent fruit and no future I can discern, seedling spawn of an overfull bear who years ago squatted a pile of peels and seeds at the dark edge of the forest.

I don't have time for you. But I need to corral that wild woody hair into some semblance of order, show you how to become a proper fruit tree, *fercryingoutloud*.

Click of decisive metal snipping thin stems waiting on spring sap, and I've tidied you up. But I'm embarrassed and walk to the next tree with the control freak straining at his leash.

ANCESTORS

~

STOOPID APPLE

Last night I could have been moving into our newly remodeled office. Instead, I sent yet another driving uppercut into the jaw of delayed gratification. I made an apple pie. These days most apple pies come from a bakery. They rarely arrive on the table with a tale. But this pie, the one newly emerged from the oven with cinnamon ooze bubbling from slits in a toasted crust, is an exclamation mark at the end of a story.

At the Johnny Gunter cabin a stocky seedling apple tree riddled with sapsucker holes stands next to the garden. The tree thrives there. I haven't asked it directly about the source of its happiness, but probably this has something to do with summer watering and fertilizer meant for the garden. Every growing season it sprouts prodigious new shoots that require most of a winter day to prune. Beginning in early August, there are buckets of green apples with red stripes. This is an unusual ripening time, an interstitial apple space between Yellow Transparents of late July and Gravensteins of early September.

My mother loves all trees. She loves this tree, too. But she detests the apple. There are good reasons for her loathing. The fruit goes from hard and green to soft and flavorless in a few days. Since we visit the cabin only once a week or so, most of the apples fall and either rot where they land or get pitched over the orchard fence to become nighttime snacks for the deer and bear. The deer and bear might be the only ones completely satisfied with this arrangement. In honor of Mom's disdain, I've given the apple the varietal name Stoopid.

One summer I started eating the Stoopid apples. This was partly because my supply of early summer apples was cut off when the decrepit Yellow Transparent finally toppled, pushed over by a huge feral cow that still roamed the valley and used the tree for a scratching post. Any apple pie in August is better than no apple pie. I discovered that by restricting the harvest to apples that are firm and just barely ripe, then immediately peeling, slicing, and coating them with sugar and cinnamon and freshly ground nutmeg, those Stoopid apples make one heck of a pie.

Uncle Johnny has been gone for three decades, and no one still living knows why he husbanded this odd apple tree. In his absence we are at once imprisoned by the loss of his actual story and free to surmise how that Stoopid apple came to be. Mom has concluded that Johnny grew the tree only to graft onto it other more respectable apple varieties. He just didn't get around to doing this. I'm not sure about this hypothesis. Johnny was an accomplished grafter, and that bastard tree has been around for a long while. If he'd wanted to graft on other varieties, he likely would have done so.

I've decided that Johnny knew exactly what he wanted from this wild hare of a tree—another pot of applesauce and one or two more pies to fill in the otherwise smooth succession of summer apples that precede the fall season. So I've continued the story of Johnny's Stoopid tree. I've made a lot of Stoopid pies, and they seem to make people happy. The deer and bear are happy with the Stoopid windfalls. The Stoopid tree is happy with my pruning and surplus water and fertilizer from the garden. I'm happy. How about a scoop of story with that Stoopid apple pie?

REMEMBERING JERRY

I can't recall with certainty when I first met Jerry Gatchell. But I do remember my first meaningful encounter with him. The Johnny Gunter cabin is about a mile down Upper Smith River Road from the Gatchell place, so one evening I stopped in on my way home. Martha was somewhere inside. Jerry was out front grilling red sweet peppers on a hibachi. The conversation was a little strained. Jerry was polite, but my sense was that he didn't want to talk to me. Even though my family had lived down the road off and on for decades, I was a stranger, a skinny coyote who looked as though he might eat him out of house and home.

Months later I bumped into Jerry and Martha at a Dennis Kucinich rally. As a newborn writer, I was so wet that I had no idea they were pillars of the local literary community. I handed Jerry my essay on the Johnny Gunter Potato, a variety he and Martha had saved for years and then reintroduced into my family. I felt as though I was endearing myself to a half-wild animal.

Over the years my stops at the Gatchell house became nearly weekly. I began to realize it was I who was half-wild. I needed the burrs brushed from my matted fur, needed to be coaxed down from my precarious perches by Jerry's reasonable and resonant bass, needed to be taught to go outside to pee. I really was a skinny coyote, omnivorous and hungry for many things.

Along with the deer, bear, bobcat, barred owls, and spotted skunks, I became a well-established and welcome part of the Gatchell community of beings. At nightfall, we pressed in from the edges of the forest and circled the evening fire out front. A spotted skunk would sometimes sneak under our legs to snitch cat kibbles. One night a skunk was deep into a discreet nighttime foray inside the house when it was surprised by the cat coming around a corner. All smell broke loose. When I arrived the following evening, a musky stench still hung heavy around the place. Jerry looked at me, cocked his green beret to one side, and pronounced "The boundary between inside and outside is getting a little fuzzy around here."

No words better capture Jerry, if ever Jerry could be captured. That deadpan delivery was a hysterical one-line manifesto for life. He loved the Lakota precept "all my relations," or "we are all related." And I realized that I still had it wrong. Jerry wasn't trying to tame me. He wanted all of us to rediscover that undomesticated quantum universe of our ancestors, open our doors to the boisterous half-wild world, the place where all boundaries are fuzzy and everything is a brotherly mess, the place where, in the rambunctious messiness of it all, a skunk could steal a little cat food, the house could end up smelly, and it would all be good fun.

When a small group of overly boisterous cells moved into Jerry's brain and began to grow with no respect for their relations, he had to move to town. The boundaries surrounding him became too rigid. Patiently, and with civility, he took his leave. In this wild quantum tangle that Jerry embraced, the place where he and the rest of us try to sort out our lives in relationship to the many other lives with whom we are joined, he asks of us one thing: that we live and die with our arms wide open to all our relations, to the Wholeness of Everything. My friend, I am going to try. You have fed me.

DR MOWER

The DR Brush Mower looks like a giant orange locust. The head is a broad, flat housing covering whirling horizontal blades turned by a belt driven by a Briggs and Stratton engine. The handles are two legs arcing upward and backward. The DR rides on a pair of skinny spoked wheels. The human operator does not ride. The human walks behind, hanging on. The DR is designed for one thing—to keep relentless biological succession from reclaiming human engineered landscapes.

The meadow below the Johnny Gunter cabin is bathed in morning dew. In the parking area I fire up the DR. Three hard pulls on the starter cord, and the engine roars across this small still valley of my maternal ancestors. I engage the mower belt, sending blades whirling across damp knapweed and dandelions covering the lower end of the meadow.

Most people don't place hard physical labor high on their list of meditative experiences. But with good ear protection, the roar of two-cycle internal combustion driving spinning blades is reduced to something akin to a large waterfall. Everyone loves a waterfall. The reverberating engine, the vibration in my arms, the exhaust, the slow sweaty walk behind those reaching handles all coalesce into an incongruous ruminating trance. This is when the questions start.

Why am I mowing? Why not let the meadow revert to the old forest it once was? My reasons are superficial: to control invasive knapweed, to lower the fire danger, to make the property look inhabited. Yes. But also: to be a good son, to be a good great-nephew of Uncle Johnny, to be a good steward of the place he left us, to gain approval from the living and dead. Yes. But also: to feel the salty seep of sweat in my armpits, the vibrating pull on my arms, to know that for me the Puritan Work Ethic is bullshit, that this ass-busting work feeds my rawest animal self with unreasoning joy.

Why am I here? Because I was born and have miraculously managed to remain alive, the oldest son of my father who will be leaving this sun-drenched earth sooner than later, my father who will be leaving me, by accident of birth order, to become the unwilling patriarch of my immediate family.

Why was I born first? In fact, I wasn't. My older brother, Tommy Glen, died over six decades ago. He was 4 months old. Tommy had congenital heart issues that caused him to struggle for oxygen, struggle even in this blue-green envelope of abundant oxygen that supports the lives of so many. *Why did you leave so quickly? Did you know deep inside your small malformed heart that you would never mow the meadow when Mom and Dad grew old? Did you know even then that I would follow, that I would revel in this sweaty strain behind the DR? Should I be grateful that you, my older brother, have left me this: the drenching sun, the rising heat, the disappearing morning dew?*

Back in the parking area, I kill the engine. My questions die in the silence. Below me, knapweed furrows the meadow in neat windrows, ready to brown in the oven of an oncoming heat wave. I stand for a moment, soaked in salty unreasoning joy.

PALINDROME

Palindrome: "a word, phrase, or sequence that reads the same backward and forward. From the Greek *palin* 'again' and *drom* 'to run'. Running back again." *Dad* is a palindrome. *T.N.T.*, my father's initials, is a palindrome, as are the numbers *313*, the room where Dad took his last breaths.

A *human being human* is a palindrome of words. But a human life is not a palindrome. It has an arrow of time: conception, birth, life, death, and along the way a hopeful accumulation of complexity, wisdom, and love. My father being human cannot be swapped *end to end to end* with something identical. His being was complex: pilot, aircraft mechanic, missile inspector, logger, trucker, businessman, mechanic (again), pilot (again), trucker (again), firefighter when needed, fixer of all things, builder of all things, brother, uncle, husband for 63 years and 5 months, father for 62 years and 3 months, grandfather, great-grandfather.

Family is not a palindrome. My father wanted a family more than anything. We became a star radiating from his core, super-heated gasses hurled outward that asserted themselves in space and time. At the end, the hot arms of our love gathered in, coalesced around Dad's center, held him gently, uproariously, solemnly, imperfectly, until he was finished being human.

Gratitude is not a palindrome but an endless sea. I am filled with it: cool pitcher of water, warm cup of coffee, syrupy bourbon on ice, silver boat of Thanksgiving gravy, thankful for my father and his being, for his family into which I was born, for his tranquil death.

Love being human being love. Because our lives on the bright surface of this planet are not palindromes. We begin. We end. We will not run back again.

CANNING WEEK

To be completely honest, I'm exhausted. All of this week, I've given my mornings and evenings over to peeling, canning, juicing, and drying apples, pears, elderberries, grapes, and tomatoes. This compulsion to preserve food is a sickness that I'm not anxious to heal. I believe in the sacredness of eating my own stuff—that it's good for body, soul, and planet—and my pantry is filling with beautiful jars of food.

Nevertheless, the week has gotten a little weird. I've been sleep deprived and late for work. This morning I didn't even take the time to pack a lunch. This meant two slices to go from Track Town Pizza down the street. I gush over good pizza. But eating out has never been a good use of planetary resources, and the irony of eating at the pizza buffet because homegrown food takes so much time is, well, delicious. Sorry, but I couldn't resist.

This week, I subjugated all creative impulses to the cause of food preservation. I haven't written a word before today. Oregon Poet Laureate Kim Stafford encourages us to engage in a daily writing practice as a way to "each day create a point of light in a dark world." I admire his wisdom. But these days my points of light are the likeness of golden honey-canned pears, blackhole bottles of elderberry juice, bubbling half-pints of pumpkin-colored salmon, and cooling jars of tomatoes the color of freshly butchered meat. Hopefully these gleaming jars of food are their own poetry.

Earlier in this marathon week of preservation, I dropped an uncapped jar of hot elderberry juice. It streamed across the kitchen floor with the heaviness of blood. The jar didn't break, but I did, an outpouring of sorrow well beyond anything justified by half a bottle of spilled juice. Luckily the wound was seeping, purple, and venous rather than pulsing, red, and arterial. After 10 minutes, I staunched the flow and got back in the game. A wise friend recently told me that we can never know when Grief will reach up from some unnamed cavern in our soul and grab us by the heart. This is Truth.

I've also grieved for Dad in my sleep. Dreams of him rushed through dim canyons of early morning, sifting and scouring the rubble and bedrock of my being. These excursions into my subconscious confuse me, so I don't spend time dwelling on them. Rather, I trust that when the rains finally come and the fish run, the gravel will be clean and ready for spawning another generation. Certainly the pantry will be well stocked.

This morning it was a relief to put away the canner.

SIFT

Ashes are lighter than love. Your sons and grandchildren sweat them across five rugged miles to this four-acre jewel of clarity held in the lap of granite crags, lofty prayer circle of shadowy spires shouldering chittering falcons. Fingers of wind reach down, ripple mirrored water. Knuckles tap gently at our lonely void, fall silent.

Ashes are darker than tufts of snowy goat hair snagged on stunted spruce, quieter than rock clatter kicked down by black hooves. Your gray drift sifts and shifts against itself.

Ashes are grittier than the shiny old photo, you with your father standing on granite slipping away into dark water, pale fingers of trout dangling between you, lake's edge lined with spruce eight decades shorter.

Ashes are drier than tears, salt rain dimpling the film of you spreading across the surface like that wildfire haze in the east. Bits of bone, denser than water, brighter than submerged rock, glitter upward like scales of large trout stalking grasshoppers in shallows.

Ashes become trout. We catch three for breakfast, fry sheets of white flesh with potatoes and onions, eat atop the same gray granite shoulder stooping into transparent water, into time. Fish become bone. You become.

SEEP OF DAYLIGHT

My eyes slid open to moonlight seeping through a thin bedroom curtain. I slipped on clogs and went outside, hoping to see a three-quarter ball setting big and orange over the western ridgetop. But there was no moon. Instead, daylight was breathing onto the browning meadow the way color returns to the face of someone newly resuscitated. Overcast draped so heavy and low that its vapor snagged on the old trees topping the north ridge. Not-quite-rain stippled my bare arms, the kind of mist that soaks the grass but only teases summer roots. From my left came the steady *pishing* of the Rain Bird sprinkler delivering the gift of spring water to chest-high corn and vining winter squash. The sprinkler is set to come on at 5 AM. Daybreak. But nothing was breaking. Instead, light was slowly bending around the curve of Earth's hip, a dawn that spread over the meadow and ridges the way a sad person smiles.

I'm grateful for this shy version of a Coast Range summer. Maybe trees won't burn, the duff won't bake, and the chanterelles will recover under autumn rains. Cooler days have left dewberries still ripe on prickled vines, and I'll be able to pick enough for a pie for the family reunion. There was even a long-lived tiger lily blooming along the roadside, speckled black on sunset orange.

But for reasons I can't name, this weather has me unsettled. It is the summer that hugs with one arm, kisses only on the cheek, commits to nothing—not rain or sun or heat or cold. This is the summer of uncertainty, or perhaps the certainty that big changes await. I have awakened from dreams that left me sad and shaken. Dad has been gone for awhile, but on the drive over, a sinkhole of grief gaped in my chest, leaving pieces of me crumbling around the edges of the abyss. I nearly had to pull the truck over. Then the hole slowly closed, like this gentle seep of daylight, this easy soak of heavy mist. They told me it would be like this. Sudden. Unexpected. Like beauty. Maybe grief is beautiful.

In the meantime, there was bad coffee to be made, berries to pick, and exams to grade. I made the coffee, postponed the grading, and went berry picking.

JAR MAN

Over the years I've grown comfortable with most of my vices. But there is one continuing problem that dogs my days, one that is utterly hopeless. I'm a jar-o-holic.

Mind you, I don't lust for just any old jar. I can chuck a plastic peanut butter or jam container into the recycling in the time it takes to say "petroleum product." It's glass jars that are my issue. I love the heft in my hand, the way they show off their contents when full, their sparkling transparency when empty and clean. I love the cycle of their lives, the filling and eating and washing and cleaning and storing and refilling. They have a permanence that stands against the crazy-making transience of our high-speed throwaway world.

The depth of my problem became evident on a trip to the Northeast to visit my son and his family. Most people my age would have been surreptitiously stowing their grandsons in their suitcase. I do love my grandsons. But I was jonesin' for a newly emptied 1-gallon pickle jar that had been hucked into the recycling bin. I was planning to stuff it with dirty clothes to make space in my luggage. Seriously.

My wife knows. She saw that small dilation of my pupils and gave me one of those looks that let me know that she knows. I am nuts for jars. The last time I came home with a case of canning quarts from our local recycling center, she very politely told me there was enough room in our overstuffed house for me or another case of jars. So I built a new shed. Three-quarters of the shelves are full of empty jars: bulging gallons for honey, half-gallons for juice, all manner of half-pints, pints, and quarts. And who doesn't need all of these in both wide- and regular-mouth configurations? It's pathological.

She started keeping an eye on me while I packed for the trip home. I was allowed to save from certain death by recycling a smaller half-gallon pickle jar with some pretty designs molded into the sides. I crammed it with dirty underwear and T-shirts. She even fished the matching lid out of the garbage. I have no idea what I'll do with this beautiful piece of glass—maybe pack it with Titus Cannellini dry beans or dried Cascade Ruby Gold Corn that I'm growing this summer over at the Smith River Memorial Garden.

There was a time when I was on a first name basis with a local woman who sold recycled glass. She made a special point of saving all her 10-ounce oyster jars just for me. She'd call when she thought there were enough piled up to warrant a trip to her place out Lorane Highway. Oyster jars are heavy walled and the perfect size for salmon and tuna and wild blackberry jam. Nearly all oysters are now sold in plastic jars, and those perfect pieces of glass won't be made again. I never hand these 10-ouncers out when we give away food for the holidays, and there are so many in the pantry that I've put them in my will. I brought one of them home from Yonkers, too.

My lust for jars came naturally. Mom is in her eighties now and is still an unrecovered jar addict. She has no intention of kicking her habit. Recently she needed some help looking for a box of copper cookware in the storage area above the pantry. I lost count of the cases of canning jars that needed to be moved to find that box of pots and pans. She chose the right person for the job. Not only did I withhold judgment, I loved those boxes of jars. Our shared jar problem could send you off into the unresolvable weeds of nature versus nurture. Let me know when you get to the bottom of it. For me, I am certain only of this: Mom knows who she raised.

SPIRITS

He pulls back cold sheets stretched on a twin bed in a corner of the room he once shared with three brothers, a room now filled with the boxed and binned accumulation of 60 years, the room he crept from one childhood night to tell her he was afraid of dying.

There are spooks here. Or more properly, ghosts. Or even more properly, spirits. There are spirits of multiple generations of good-natured mongrel dogs, cats wily and tough enough to die of old age, chickens who laid down their lives in nest boxes or were eaten by raccoons, cows who gave birth to heifers and to bulls who became steers who became steaks (she always disliked that the boys named them), the bitchy old mare who taught them to ride but only when she felt like it, milk goats who became pets, pigs who would have become pets but instead were transformed into the finest bacon any of them had ever tasted, big Douglas-firs who died slow deaths from the top down and were sawed and split into firewood, and pickups whose quiet bodies rust in the pasture. There is the spirit of his grandmother who died in this room, perhaps in this very bed, and of his father only recently passed, the strongest presence of them all.

This place is thick with spirits. Their particular manifestation makes little difference. They might live only as the smoke of memory, thinning, wavering, conforming to the shape of time. They might spread across floors like warm syrup on buttermilk pancakes, ply the rooms on steamy thermals of morning coffee, or rise on a chorus of frogs from the black February pond. All that matters is this: the spirits of a place are gifts. They are not afraid to die.

WONDERING

Screech Owl sent a quavering late-night call through my bedroom window that sounded like "blackberries now." Screech Owls don't sound anything like "blackberries now," which just shows that it's all in the ear of the receiver. In any case, I found my way into the Coast Range for a very late Armenian blackberry harvest. The berries were musky and soft and would make lovely wine. September squished through my fingers and became purple juice that dribbled into the heart line of my palms.

Picking is good for wondering, a synonym for pondering, which rhymes with wandering. I wondered aimlessly in my head, through the withered end-days of summer and into autumn. There was a time when I had an abbreviated list of autumn loves: crisp days, low humidity, harvest time, hardwood colors. But I've come to love everything about autumn: the way contracting daylight ratchets down onto my upper chest, stirring late summer butterflies upward into my throat, the smoky withering anticipation of rain. But most of all I love the boisterous sadness: gray rains that bring mushrooms bursting upward to breed and die and rot, salmon bursting upstream to breed and die and rot, crickets bursting into stridulating song to breed and die and rot.

And oh, good grief, the loss. My grandson, who tasted seven different berries in a single day, has returned to his home far away. My friend Jerry and my father have left forever. Say that again. Good grief. I mean that. Because I love the loss, too, the reminders that summer and blackberries and mushrooms and salmon and crickets and the lovely colors of hardwoods and my loved ones and I are only temporary.

Fall is flexing its seasonal bicep. The rains lie somewhere beyond the southwestern horizon. When those pricks of falling water begin, I will walk outside, tilt my face to the sky, let the first drops disappear into the wet pink of my tongue. Sticky blackberry-stained palms will turn upward to be washed clean. Shall we live boisterously onward?